ETF Mastery

Diversifying Your Portfolio for Financial Success

Table of Contents

Chapter 1. Introduction

In the dynamic world of investing, the ability to diversify and enhance your portfolio is arguably one of the most valuable skills you can master. Our Special Report, "ETF Mastery: Diversifying Your Portfolio for Financial Success", offers you the key to unlock that mastery. This vivid and engaging guide sweeps away the complexities and delves into the practical strategies of successful ETF investing, empowering you to manage your assets with confidence and intelligence alike. If the notion of maximizing the potential of your financial future brings a sparkle to your eyes, then this motivating and illuminating report might just be the investment you've been waiting to make. Don't be left behind; seize control of your financial destiny today!

Chapter 2. Unlocking the Secrets of ETFs

Exchange-traded funds (ETFs) are revolutionizing the investment world. From their inception in the early 1990s, ETFs have evolved into one of the most popular investment vehicles due to their unique structure, versatility, and cost-effectiveness. Their continued growth and emergence are fueling a distinct shift in the investment landscape.

2.1. The Basics of ETFs

ETFs are investment funds traded on stock exchanges, much like individual stocks. They hold assets such as stocks, bonds, or commodities and seek to replicate the performance of specific indices or sectors. Unlike mutual funds, which are only priced at the end of each trading day, ETFs offer continuous pricing throughout the trading hours. This dynamic pricing allows for increased flexibility, offering investors the opportunity to buy or sell ETF shares at any point during the market trading hours.

ETFs also exhibit inherent tax efficiency due to their unique 'in-kind' creation and redemption process. This mechanism allows the ETF to limit capital gain distributions, thereby reducing the investor's tax liability. As a result, the after-tax return of ETFs often surpasses that of comparable mutual funds.

Another advantage of ETFs lies in their transparency. Unlike mutual funds, ETFs disclose their holdings daily. This daily disclosure helps increase their appeal for investors who prefer to have a clearer understanding of where their money is invested.

2.2. Understanding the Types of ETFs

While the basic premise of an ETF is straightforward, this investment vehicle comes in various types, each with its own set of objectives, risks, and potential returns.

1. **Index ETFs**: These are the most common type of ETFs and seek to replicate the performance of a specific index, such as the S&P 500. They offer investors a low-cost way to diversify and gain exposure to different markets.

2. **Sector ETFs**: These ETFs focus on specific sectors of the economy, such as technology, healthcare, or finance. They allow investors to target their investments towards sectors they foresee as being particularly profitable or to hedge against sectors they perceive as risky.

3. **Commodity ETFs**: These ETFs invest in physical commodities like gold, oil, or agricultural products. They provide an easy way for investors to gain exposure to commodity prices without investing directly in futures contracts.

4. **Bond ETFs**: These ETFs invest in bonds and other debt securities, offering a more stable and income-generating alternative to stock ETFs.

5. **International ETFs**: These ETFs offer exposure to international, foreign country or region-focused equity markets. They are an effortless way for investors to diversify their portfolios geographically.

6. **Inverse ETFs**: These ETFs aim to profit from a decline in the value of an underlying benchmark. They are essentially shorting the index and can act as a hedge against downturns.

7. **Leveraged ETFs**: These ETFs use financial derivatives and debt to amplify the returns of an underlying index. They are typically

used by sophisticated investors due to their high-risk nature.

2.3. Building a Portfolio with ETFs

The ability to diversify effortlessly is one of the main attractions of ETFs. By understanding your investment goals, risk tolerance, and time horizon, you can build a well-rounded portfolio using a combination of the different types of ETFs.

For many investors, index ETFs serve as the foundation of their portfolio due to their broad market exposure and low fees. Sector ETFs can also be used tactically to tilt the portfolio towards specific sectors that are expected to outperform. International ETFs play a crucial role in achieving international diversification, while bond ETFs can add a stabilizing factor to your portfolio due to their reduced volatility compared to equities.

Moreover, commodity ETFs offer a hedge against inflation risks and currency depreciation. Inverse and leveraged ETFs, though potentially riskier, can be used to hedge against market downturns or capitalize on short-term market movements, respectively.

2.4. Risk Management in ETF Investing

Every investment comes with risk, and ETFs are no exception. Managing risk is a critical aspect of successful ETF investing.

Firstly, it's important to understand that while ETFs offer diversification, this does not guarantee protection against losses. Diversification is about reducing non-systemic risk (risk linked to one particular asset), but systemic risk (risk linked to the overall market) remains. This makes it essential to align your ETF investments with your overall risk profile.

Secondly, while ETFs offer opportunities for both short-term and long-term investment strategies, investors must avoid speculative trading. Remember, the primary advantage of ETFs is their low cost, but frequent trading can result in substantial transaction costs which can erode your returns over time.

Lastly, as with all investments, understanding the underlying assets within the ETF is critical. For example, sector-specific and international ETFs may carry risks linked to those specific sectors or countries. Adequate research and due diligence are must before investing.

Thus, unlocking the secrets of ETFs begins with understanding their structure, types, and benefits, along with the risks involved. A well-planned ETF investment strategy can be a doorway to diversified, cost-effective, and flexible investing, empowering you to take control of your financial destiny.

Chapter 3. The ABCs of Diversification: Spreading Your Investments

In order to diversify a portfolio effectively, it is necessary to understand the underlying principles of diversification. At its most basic, diversification is a risk management strategy that combines a variety of investments within a portfolio. The rationale behind this technique is that a portfolio constructed of diverse investments will, on average, yield higher returns and pose a lower risk than any individual investment found within the portfolio.

Before we get started on the nuts and bolts operation of diversification, let's illustrate some key concepts that should be readily understood:

3.1. The Importance of Variance

In the world of investment, 'variance' is a statistical measurement of the dispersion of returns for a particular security or market index. Commonly used by both analysts and investors, variance provides a comprehensive view of the security's or market index's price movements below and above the mean, which is crucial when assessing volatility and investment risk. The degree of variance offers insight into the difference in potential performance between the investment being evaluated and others in its class. In diversification, variance plays a significant role, since investments behaving differently can be combined to reduce overall portfolio risk.

3.2. Correlation as a Key Ingredient

Correlation measures how different securities move in relation to each other. It is ranged from -1 to 1. When two assets have a correlation of 1, they move in perfect tandem; a correlation of -1 means they move in exact opposite directions. Investments with a correlation of zero move in a completely random, nonsynchronous manner. Understanding correlation helps in selecting non-correlated assets to diversify a portfolio and mitigate risk.

3.3. The Adage of "Don't Put All Eggs in One Basket"

This saying perfectly summarizes the principle of diversification. By spreading your investments across various types of assets, sectors, markets and currencies, you can safeguard your portfolio against severe losses. If one investment performs poorly, others may perform well and offset the loss.

3.4. Diversification and Expected Returns

In general, the objective of diversification is not necessarily to boost performance—although it can certainly help. Rather, the primary goal is to limit the impact of volatility on a portfolio. While reducing unwanted risk, diversification also provides the potential for improved returns for the level of risk that you are willing to accept.

3.5. Sector Diversification

To start with, looking at sector diversification may offer a strong foundation to portfolio diversification. An investor can divide investments across different sectors, such as technology, energy, healthcare, or consumer goods. This bodes well as sectors often behave differently under varying economic circumstances. Some sectors outperform others during different economic stages, resulting in a 'sector rotation'. Holding securities from different sectors can lead to a more stable portfolio performance over time.

3.6. Geographic Diversification

Different economies react differently to varied economic phenomena, such as changes in currency exchange rates or commodity prices. By investing in different countries and regions, one can potentially benefit from these differences. Diversification on a geographical scale involves spreading your investments across various markets, both domestic and international.

3.7. Asset Class Diversification

Different types of assets—stocks, bonds, real estate, commodities, or cash equivalents—usually perform differently at different times. By spreading investments across these assets, you can temper risk. For instance, fixed-income securities like bonds can serve as a counterweight to the more volatile equities in your portfolio.

3.8. Time Diversification

Time diversification refers to the strategy of spreading out your investments over time. This approach, also known as dollar cost averaging, can be particularly useful when investing a lump sum. Instead of investing all the money at once, which is risky because of potential fluctuations, it is allocated on a regular basis over a period.

While it's clear that investing across a variety of asset types, sectors, geographic regions, and time can reduce certain risks, it is equally crucial to consider how these parts interact. No diversification strategy meets the needs of all investors, so it's vital to develop a plan that aligns with your goals, risk tolerance, time horizon, and financial situation.

Chapter 4. Building Blocks: Analyzing Your Financial Goals

Before you begin constructing your portfolio, it is crucial to take time to consider your financial goals. These goals will provide a roadmap for your investment decisions, directing your choices in alignment with your desired outcomes. Having clear, quantifiable, and achievable financial goals is the bedrock upon which your entire investment strategy should rest.

4.1. Personal Financial Assessment

The first step in analyzing your financial goals involves a comprehensive personal financial assessment. Start by calculating your total assets, including savings accounts, real estate, business ventures, stocks, bonds, retirement accounts, and any other significant items of value. Subtract all your liabilities, like loans, mortgages, credit card balances, to determine your net worth. Understanding your asset to liability ratio provides a real-world snapshot of your current financial standing.

Next, determine your annual income and contrast it against your living expenses. This includes expenses such as rent/mortgage payment, food, utilities, insurance, and other bills. This will help you to understand your monthly cash flow and gauge the portion you can comfortably dedicate to new investments without straining financially.

Finally, prepare a risk profile. This is a measure of your capacity to withstand potential losses. Your risk appetite will be influenced by factors such as your age, income, financial expertise, and the nature of your financial goals.

4.2. Defining Your Financial Goals

Once you've completed your financial assessment, you can start defining your financial goals. These goals can range from short-term objectives like saving for a vacation or paying off your credit card debt, to long-term goals like financing your child's education or planning for retirement.

For each goal, ask yourself the following: What is the total amount required? When will you need the money? What is the duration for reaching this goal? What tools will you use to reach it? What level of risk are you comfortable taking? By answering these questions, you can map out a detailed plan for each financial goal, taking into consideration each goal's deadline, risk requirement, and investment vehicle.

4.3. Priority Setting and Time Horizons

It's likely that you have more than one financial goal, which necessitates prioritizing your objectives. Prioritization is typically based on the time horizon. Short-term goals (anything needed within five years) are usually the most urgent, followed by medium-term goals (five to ten years), and then long-term goals (more than ten years).

This arrival point is an important factor in selecting suitable investment vehicles. Short-term goals might be best served with lower-risk, liquid investments such as money market funds or Treasury Bills, while longer-term goals can bear more aggressive investing in stocks or equity ETFs.

Also remember, your financial goals will mature and change over time. Annual review of your goals and investment strategy is a prudent practice, ensuring the plan is still pertinent and aligned to your financial needs.

4.4. Diversification and Asset Allocation

ETFs make diversification and asset allocation an accessible strategy for individual investors. Diversification is achieved by holding a broad spectrum of investments from different asset classes. This strategy helps reduce the risk associated with volatility in one asset class.

Asset allocation involves the practice of dividing investment capital among different asset classes such as stocks, bonds, and cash equivalents, following a plan that reflects your individual risk tolerance, goals, and investment time horizon.

Your overall asset allocation should be favorable to your financial goals. For example, if you're aiming for a long-term goal with a high risk-tolerance, a large portion of your portfolio may be in equity ETFs. Conversely, short-term goals with low risk-tolerance may be better suited to bond ETFs or money market funds.

4.5. Investment Instruments: Introduction to ETFs

Exchange Traded Funds (ETFs) are a compelling choice for diversification and asset allocation. They are designed to track the performance of a specific index, sector, commodity, or asset class. By encapsulating a diverse array of holdings, they provide instant access to a wide variety of markets, industries, and asset classes.

Apart from diversification, ETFs also provide liquidity, as they can be bought and sold like individual stocks. They offer transparency, with their holdings being disclosed daily, and low expense ratios, as most

ETFs are passively managed, tracking a pre-defined index.

4.6. Establishing an Investment Strategy

Your financial goals will largely dictate your investment strategy. This strategy should specify what percentage of your portfolio will be assigned to various asset classes such as stocks, bonds, and cash or cash equivalents. It should also lay out your ETF selection strategy. Here, element considerations are the ETF's underlying index or asset class, historic performance, expense ratio, issuer reputation, and liquidity.

With your financial goals as an anchor, your investment strategy will guide your buying and selling decisions. This includes when to enter a position, when to exit, and when to stay put. Each decision should be systematically evaluated against your financial goals and investment strategy.

By putting in the effort to fully analyze your financial goals, you can create a robust, personalized plan for your investments. ETFs offer a flexible tool for executing that strategy, allowing you to diversify your holdings and control risk in your portfolio. With careful planning, due diligence, and ongoing management, you can make confident and informed decisions, which can lead to financial success.

Chapter 5. Decoding the Language of ETFs: A Glossary for Investors

In the landscape of investment, Exchange Traded Funds (ETFs) represent one of the most crucial and versatile components. Made unique by their structure and function, ETFs offer numerous opportunities for investors. However, to make the most out of ETFs, it's important to understand the language of this investment domain. Let's dive into some of those vital terminologies.

5.1. The Basics: ETF Definitions

When it comes to ETFs, there are a handful of critical terms every investor should be familiar with:

1. **Exchange-Traded Fund (ETF)**: An investment fund traded on stock exchanges, much like stocks. It holds assets such as stocks, bonds, or commodities and aims to track a specific index while offering the flexibility of intraday trading.

2. **Intraday Trading**: The buying and selling of ETF shares within the same trading day. Unlike mutual funds, ETF shares can be traded throughout the day at fluctuating prices.

3. **Underlying Index**: This is the benchmark which the ETF aims to track. Each ETF uses a specific index as its model, striving to replicate its performance.

4. **Net Asset Value (NAV)**: A measure of the value of the fund's total assets minus its liabilities, divided by the number of outstanding shares.

5.2. Understanding Asset Classes & Types of ETFs

In ETF investing, there are significant terminologies used to describe various asset classes and ETF types.

1. **Equity ETFs**: These funds invest in stocks of corporations. They are the most common type of ETF.

2. **Bond ETFs**: These ETFs invest in bonds and other debt securities. They could be corporate bonds, government bonds, municipal bonds, etc.

3. **Commodity ETFs**: These ETFs mainly invest in commodities like gold, silver, oil, etc.

4. **Sector and Industry ETFs**: These are ETFs that target specific sectors (e.g. technology, health) or industries (e.g. semiconductor, biotech) within the economy.

5. **International and Global ETFs**: These ETFs invest in non-domestic securities, offering investors a convenient way to gain international exposure.

5.3. Delving into Costs and Payments

In ETF investing, understanding the associated costs and potential returns is vital. Here are some associated glossary terms:

1. **Expense Ratio**: Represents the cost to run the ETF, expressed as a percentage of the fund's total assets.

2. **Dividends**: These are payments made by an ETF to its shareholders, representing a portion of the earnings from the fund's underlying investments.

3. **Capital Gains Distribution**: This occurs when the ETF sells off any of its holdings at a profit. The gain is distributed to the

shareholders of the ETF.

4. **Yield**: It refers to the income return on an investment, such as interest or dividends received, and is usually expressed as an annual percentage based on the investment's cost or current market value.

5.4. Getting Technical: Advanced Terminologies

For the sophisticated investor, there are more complex terminologies that form the advanced language of ETFs.

1. **Leveraged ETFs**: These ETFs use financial derivatives and debt to amplify the returns of an underlying index.

2. **Inverse ETFs**: Designed to perform as the inverse of the index or benchmark it tracks. Essentially, it will gain value if the index declines.

3. **Tracking Error**: It is the difference between the return on an ETF and the return on the benchmark index it's supposed to be tracking.

5.5. Mastering Trading and Liquidity Terms

Several terms are specifically related to the trading and liquidity of ETFs.

1. **Bid-Ask Spread**: The difference between the highest price that a buyer is willing to pay for an ETF share (bid), and the lowest price that a seller is willing to accept (ask).

2. **Premium/Discount**: An ETF is said to be trading at a premium when its market price is higher than its Net Asset Value (NAV),

and at a discount when its market price is lower than its NAV.

3. **Creation Unit**: It is a specific block of ETF shares (generally 50,000), created or redeemed at the request of large institutional investors.

These are just some of the many terms you'll encounter in the intricate sphere of ETFs. The mastery of this vocabulary will not only aid your understanding but also empower you to make informed investment decisions. With each term acting as a piece of the wider puzzle, a comprehensive knowledge of these glossaries will enable an investor to leverage the advantages offered by ETFs, thereby diversifying and enhancing one's portfolio.

Chapter 6. Emerging Markets vs Developed Markets: Where to place your bets

Emerging and developed markets offer different opportunities and risks for investors. The key to understanding where to place your bets starts with an in-depth comprehension of these markets.

There are numerous factors to consider when deciding where to invest. This includes assessing the economic climate, the political stability, the business environment, and the market's maturity. It's also important to gauge the potential returns, considering not only the potential for high growth but also the risk involved.

6.1. Emerging Markets: An Overview

Emerging markets are countries that are progressing towards becoming advanced economies. They are characterized by rapid economic growth and liberalization, but they are also typified by volatility.

Countries considered to be emerging markets include China, India, Brazil, and South Africa, among others. These countries have made substantial strides towards liberalizing their economies and have shown significant growth in recent years.

Investing in emerging markets can offer significant rewards due to the potential for high growth rates. These markets usually provide lucrative opportunities for investors willing to accept the accompanying risk.

6.2. Developed Markets: An Overview

On the other hand, developed markets are characterized by strong, well-regulated economies. They typically have high income per capita and are highly industrialized. These economies include the United States, Germany, the UK, and Japan, among others.

Investing in developed markets means investing in mature economies that offer stability, predictable growth rates, and lower risk. These markets offer investor protection, largely due to stringent regulations, and are characterized by transparency, efficiency, and liquidity.

6.3. Factors to Consider

When deciding where to invest, certain determining factors come into play. These factors can have a huge impact on the profitability and risk profile of your investments.

1. **Economic Growth and Stability:** Emerging markets often offer higher growth rates than developed markets. However, this growth can be unpredictable and comes with a higher level of risk.

2. **Risk Levels:** Developed markets are characterized by lower levels of risk due to their stability and well-regulated nature.

3. **Investor Protection:** Laws and regulations for investor protection tend to be well-developed and enforced in developed markets, but this may not be the case in all emerging markets.

4. **Profitability:** While emerging markets can offer high yields, they can also come with high risk. Developed markets offer a lower yield, but with more stability and reliability.

6.4. Moving Beyond the Traditional Definition

Recent years have seen the lines blurred between emerging and developed markets. The likes of South Korea and Taiwan have often been categorized as emerging markets but exhibit traits similar to developed markets.

Such economies have transitioned towards being more service-oriented and have well-regulated, efficient, and transparent financial markets. They often show lower levels of political and economic risk compared to traditional emerging markets, yet they provide higher growth rates than developed market economies.

6.5. Strategies for Investing

Choosing where to invest is not about choosing one market over the other. A successful investment strategy is about achieving a balanced, diversified portfolio.

1. **Diversification:** A mix of investments across both market types can help to balance risk and return.

2. **Understanding Market Cycles:** Both emerging and developed markets have economic cycles. Knowing where a country is in its cycle can help when deciding when and where to invest.

3. **Staying Informed:** Markets are dynamic and conditions can change quickly. Regularly reviewing and adjusting your portfolio is key.

4. **Working with Professionals:** Investment professionals or financial advisors can provide helpful guidance and expertise.

In conclusion, both emerging and developed markets offer unique opportunities for investors. Striking the right balance between the two can help create an investment portfolio that leverages high-growth opportunities while maintaining stability for long-term profitability.

Chapter 7. Sector ETFs: The Key to Industry-Specific Investing

In the labyrinthine realm of investing, Sector ETFs serve as a powerful tool that allows investors to gain exposure to specific industry sectors within the overall economy. As a well-seasoned financier, you would understand the imperative to diversify and not keep all your financial eggs in one basket. Sector ETFs can assist in immeasurably by providing directed access to the financial performance of assorted industries.

7.1. An Introduction to Sector ETFs

Sector Exchange Traded Funds, or Sector ETFs, function as a type of investment vehicle that allows you to invest in a specific sector, or industry, of the market. These can range from technology, to health care, to energy, among others. Herein lies the beauty of Sector ETFs - they let you custom tailor your portfolio to reflect your individual financial objectives and risk tolerance.

Each ETF is a collection of securities, which could include stocks, bonds, or commodities, that align with a particular sector. The value of an ETF is linked to the performance of the underlying assets, therefore enabling operational diversification. Herein, Sector ETFs offer the rare occasion for niche investing, allowing you an acute sense of control over what you are investing in, without having to buy each security individually.

7.2. Understanding the Purpose and Role of Sector ETFs

Sector ETFs allow investors to gain precise exposure to individual sectors or industries, often referred to as 'vertical investing'. This single-sector focus affords the possibility of accruing significant returns if the sector performs well. For savvy investors anticipating growth in certain sectors, this can prove to be a lucrative strategy.

The purpose of Sector ETFs, therefore, can be multi-fold. You can utilise them for speculative purposes, betting on the predicted booming industry. Alternatively, they can be effectively employed as a defensive manoeuvre in volatile markets, to invest in sectors reputed for their stability during thunderous times. They can also be used to generate income through dividends in sectors that are known for high dividend pay-outs, like utilities.

7.3. Identifying the Benefits of Sector ETFs

Investing through Sector ETFs provide several advantages. The most noted benefits include targeted exposure, diversification, dividend income, cost-effectiveness and ample liquidity.

1. **Targeted Exposure**: Sector ETFs offer concentrated exposure to a specific industry of your choosing. This provides the opportunity to strategically capitalize on growth trends in industries that have a strong upside potential.

2. **Diversification**: Sector ETFs allow for the easy inclusion of a wide range of sectors in your portfolio, aiding to decrease overarching investment risk.

3. **Dividend Income**: Certain Sector ETFs, reflecting sectors renowned for paying high dividends, could generate substantial

income for investors.

4. **Cost-effectiveness**: Buying each stock of a sector separately could be a costly endeavour, while investing in a Sector ETF tracking the sector encapsulates cost efficiency.

5. **Liquidity**: ETFs are traded like stocks on an exchange, meaning they bring with them a high degree of liquidity and flexibility.

7.4. Selecting and Investing in Sector ETFs

Choosing the right Sector ETFs largely depends on your individual investment goals, risk tolerance and time horizon. Still, a few general tips can streamline this process.

1. **Research and Analyze**: Understand the sector you're interested in and its future growth prospects. Consider factors such as industry trends, market conditions, and economic indicators, to name a few.

2. **Evaluate the ETF**: Scrutinize the underlying holdings, expense ratios, the fund's performance history and the credibility of its management.

3. **Diversify**: To reduce potential risk, consider diversifying across several sectors that have low correlation to each other.

4. **Monitor your investments**: Regularly supervise your portfolio's performance, making adjustments as per market shits and your ever-evolving financial goals.

7.5. Drawbacks and Risks of Sector ETFs

Although Sector ETFs present numerous perks, like all investment mechanisms, they come with their share of pitfalls. These primarily include the exposure to sector-specific risks, increased volatility due to a concentrated focus on a single industry and the potential for a lack of diversification if only a few Sector ETFs are chosen.

Always be wary of these risks; conduct due diligence and, if required, seek guidance from a qualified financial advisor before making your investment decision.

In conclusion, Sector ETFs can prove to be an incredibly efficient and effective tool for both diversification and deliberate, targeted investment. While they do come with their set of risks, mindful investing—backed by diligent research—can substantially mitigate these hazards, allowing you to fully harness the potential of sector-specific investing.

Chapter 8. Risk Tolerance and Portfolio Construction: The Fine Art of Balance

Understanding and managing risk is a crucial part of investing, and it all starts with a self-assessment: determining your level of risk tolerance. Your risk tolerance is your comfort level with the potentials for losses, in pursuit of gains. It depends on numerous factors, including your income, savings, financial goals, and even your emotional disposition towards potential losses.

8.1. Defining Risk Tolerance

Your risk tolerance can be defined as the degree of variability in investment returns that you're willing to withstand. It's an essential aspect of investing since it shapes the scope and limits of your investment strategy. Understanding your risk tolerance will allow you to align your portfolio with your investment goals and comfort level.

There are two broad categories of risk tolerance: high and low. If you have high-risk tolerance, you can afford to potentially lose capital in the short term, in hopes of more substantial long-term gains. Conversely, if you have low-risk tolerance, consistency and capital preservation are more important than sizable gains, and you prefer less volatile, reputable investments.

Yet, risk tolerance is not static. It changes with life circumstances such as age, income, and financial responsibilities.

8.2. Testing Your Risk Tolerance

Several tools can help you determine your risk tolerance, including questionnaires, software applications, and financial advisors. Each of these tools will run you through different scenarios that project potential losses or gains in given circumstances.

The size of your investments, the potential of losing some or all of it, and how you'd react to such a situation extensively determine your risk tolerance. The objective of these tools is to simulate these situations, observe your psychological response, and subsequently estimate your risk tolerance.

But remember, these tools and the resultant readings are just starting points. As your circumstances evolve, regularly reassess your risk tolerance to stay in line with your current reality.

8.3. Portfolio Construction

Having defined and understood your risk tolerance, the next step is portfolio construction. This process melds together your investment strategy with your risk tolerance. If done right, you will be able to wade through market volatility without going beyond your comfort zone.

To construct a portfolio, you need to follow a process, which broadly includes:

1. Setting clear investment goals

2. Identifying an appropriate asset allocation

3. Selecting securities to incorporate into the portfolio

The first crucial ingredient is setting clear and measurable financial goals. Whether it's to save for a home, college tuition, retirement, or simply wealth accumulation, defining your goals allows you to work towards them accurately.

After defining your goals, the second step is asset allocation. Deciding on the mix of different asset classes (equities, bonds, commodities, etc.) according to your risk tolerance dictates your portfolio's potential return and risk characteristics. While high-risk investors may lean towards equities, low-risk investors would prefer bonds or other fixed income securities.

The last step in portfolio construction is selecting individual securities. This step is often the most complex, as it involves thorough research to identify sound investment opportunities that align with the risk and return characteristics of your portfolio.

8.4. Balancing Risk and Reward

The art of portfolio construction significantly relies on striking a balance between risk and reward. Based on your risk tolerance, you need to strategically distribute your investments across various asset classes to minimize risk and maximize potential returns. This is also known as diversification.

Portfolios that lean towards a single asset class are exposed to higher risk. For example, an all-stock portfolio might offer potentially high returns, but it becomes vulnerable during a market downturn. On the other hand, an all-bond portfolio might help preserve capital, but it may not yield sufficient returns to surpass inflation or meet investment goals.

To strike a balance, the key is diversifying across asset classes and within asset classes. This versatile approach allows your portfolio to absorb market shocks, deliver steady returns, and align with your risk tolerance.

Remember, diversification doesn't guarantee a profit, and it doesn't protect against losses in a declining market. But it does provide the possibility of both reducing risk and achieving consistent returns over the long term.

8.5. Ongoing Portfolio Assessment

Your work isn't done once your portfolio is constructed. Regular and ongoing assessment is required to ensure your portfolio maintains the risk-reward balance. You must reassess your portfolio at least annually or whenever major life changes occur.

Changes in the market, your financial situation, or your goals might necessitate portfolio adjustments. This process of adjusting your portfolio is known as rebalancing, which involves buying or selling assets to return your portfolio to its target asset allocation.

In conclusion, the relationship between risk tolerance and portfolio construction is inherently intimate. Mastering your risk tolerance aids in making informed decisions during portfolio construction, thus striking that delicate balance between risk and reward. To navigate the choppy waters of the financial markets, understand your risk tolerance, construct your portfolio to mirror it, regularly monitor its performance, and adjust it as needed. By so doing, you're not just investing; you're investing wisely.

Chapter 9. Index Funds vs ETFs: A Comparative Analysis

Many investors grapple with the decision between investing in Index Funds and ETFs (Exchange Traded Funds). Both financial instruments offer unique advantages, and they share some striking similarities as well. In this chapter, we're going to embark on a detailed comparative analysis of Index Funds and ETFs to help you make an informed decision for your investment repertoire.

9.1. Understanding the Basics

Let's start by understanding the basic concepts. Index funds are types of mutual funds which aim to replicate the performance of a specific index. By investing in an index fund, investors can achieve a diversification similar to that of the index, without owning individual securities.

On the other hand, ETFs are traded on the stock market similar to stocks, and can be bought or sold throughout the trading day at fluctuating prices. Like index funds, most ETFs aim to track the performance of a specific index, offering investors exposure to a diversified portfolio of securities that make up that index.

9.2. Diversification and Risk

Both index funds and ETFs offer investors a high level of diversification, a vital aspect in mitigating risk. By investing in many securities at once, the risks associated with individual investments are spread throughout the portfolio, insulating the fund holder from catastrophic losses.

However, there are still fundamental differences. Index funds typically involve lower levels of risk compared to ETFs due to their unique trading mechanics. ETFs' trade-like stocks lend themselves to increased market risk, including flash crashes and short selling. Additionally, traders using leverage or sophisticated trading strategies with ETFs might find themselves facing higher levels of risk than more conservative index fund investors.

9.3. Liquidity and Trading Flexibility

ETFs are highly liquid and can be traded throughout the day at market prices, similar to individual stocks. This presents an advantage for active traders who need flexibility to swiftly enter or exit positions.

Index funds, on the other hand, only allow for buying or selling at the end of the trading day, at a price equal to the fund's Net Asset Value (NAV) determined after market close. For those with a long-term investment strategy who prioritize stability over real-time trading, this limitation may not be detrimental.

9.4. Cost Analysis

When it comes to cost, the structure of index funds and ETFs could lead to variations. Index funds stand out for their low expense ratios, as they simply replicate the components of the index and are passively managed. However, ETFs tend to have an advantage when it comes to tax efficiency due to the "in-kind" creation and redemption process, which helps limit taxable capital gain distributions.

Furthermore, ETFs might have additional indirect costs due to their trade-like stocks nature. For instance, investors might need to pay a spread or commission when buying and selling ETF units.

9.5. Dividends

In the realm of dividends, ETFs typically offer more flexibility. Investors may choose to have dividends automatically reinvested or distributed as cash into their account. This can prove advantageous for income-focused investors. Index funds typically reinvest dividends automatically, which may not meet the requirements of investors who seek regular income from their investments.

9.6. Tailoring to Investment Goals

An astute investor must primarily base their choice of investment vehicles on their unique goals, strategies, and risk tolerance. As a general rule, if you want the flexibility of intraday trading and dividends flexibility, ETFs are typically a suitable option. If your focus is on long-term, buy-and-hold investment with low costs and stability, index funds might be the better route.

In conclusion, the question of whether to choose Index Funds or ETFs is not a matter of absolute superiority, but of how well these financial instruments align with your investing approach and goals. While there are significant differences, both index funds and ETFs have the potential to be powerful tools for diversifying your portfolio. Understanding their individual characteristics, benefits, and potential disadvantages will empower you to make informed investment decisions.

Remember that investment involves risk, and it's crucial to conduct thorough research and perhaps consult with an investment advisor before deciding the best path for you. Make your choice wisely, and you'll be well on your way towards mastering your financial destiny.

Chapter 10. The Role of ETFs in Retirement Planning

Exchange-traded funds, or ETFs, have emerged as a popular and efficient instrument for investors seeking diversified exposure to a particular asset class, sector, or index. A proper understanding of how these financial products function, their potential benefits, and associated risks make them an invaluable tool, especially in the context of retirement planning.

10.1. Understanding ETFs

ETFs are investment funds that trade on stock exchanges just like an individual company stock. They are typically designed to track the performance of specific indexes, providing investors with broad market exposure. However, ETFs are not confined to market indexes and can also be sector-specific, commodity-based, or revolve around a particular investment theme.

Being composed of multiple securities which may include stocks, bonds, or commodities, ETFs afford inherent diversification. This advantage can be further leveraged to create a balanced investment portfolio that aligns with your risk parameters and financial goals.

10.2. The ETF Advantage in Retirement Planning

For long-term investors, such as those planning for retirement, ETFs offer several potential benefits.

1. **Diversification**: ETFs can offer broad market or specific sector exposure, mitigating the risk associated with investing heavily in single stock or bond.

2. **Flexibility**: Unlike traditional mutual funds, ETFs can be bought or sold during market hours at prevailing market prices. This gives investors greater control over their investment timing.

3. **Cost-effectiveness**: ETFs typically have lower expense ratios than actively managed funds since most ETFs are index funds.

4. **Transparency**: The holdings of each ETF are disclosed daily, so you always know what assets you own through your ETF.

A retirement portfolio can benefit from these characteristics, serving both the accumulation and decumulation phases of retirement effectively.

10.3. Building a Retirement Portfolio with ETFs

The first step in leveraging ETFs for retirement planning is understanding your investment goals, risk tolerance, and time horizon.

1. **Establish Retirement Objectives**: Determine what you want your retirement to look like. Calculate the amount you need in your nest egg to sustain your anticipated lifestyle.

2. **Assess your Risk Tolerance**: This includes your ability to weather financial loss and the level of volatility you can endure in your portfolio. Remember, as you near retirement, your risk capacity typically diminishes.

3. **Time Horizon**: Your investment horizon is likely to shift as you approach retirement, which may necessitate a switch from more aggressive growth-oriented ETFs to income-focused or capital preservation ETFs.

Once your investment profile is established, the next step is ETF selection.

10.4. ETF Selection for Retirement

The wide array of ETFs available can cater to practically every conceivable investment need. It's advisable to follow a disciplined approach and pick ETFs that align best with your retirement objectives.

1. **Equity ETFs**: Suitable for younger investors with a high-risk tolerance, seeking capital growth. These ETFs track various stock market indexes and their performance is tied directly to the overall stock market.

2. **Fixed Income ETFs**: Particularly useful for those nearing or in retirement. These ETFs hold bond investments, offering lower risk and consistent income.

3. **Dividend ETFs**: Focus on companies that have a strong history of paying dividends. They can generate regular income and are suitable for those seeking both income and growth.

4. **International ETFs**: Provide exposure to foreign markets, hence offering added diversification.

5. **Sector-Specific ETFs**: Allow you to target specific sectors of the economy when you expect them to outperform.

Here it's key to balance between growth (equity ETFs, sector-specific ETFs, international ETFs), income (dividend ETFs, fixed income ETFs), and risk management (mixture of all, with the proportion depending on your risk tolerance).

10.5. Adjusting Your ETF Portfolio Over Time

An ETF retirement portfolio isn't a set and forget type of investment. As you transit through different stages of life, your financial needs and goals witness changes, which should be mirrored in your portfolio.

Up until the accumulation phase, your portfolio might be heavily tilted towards equity ETFs, facilitating capital growth. As you transition into your retirement, rebalancing towards more income-oriented and lower risk bond ETFs will serve to protect your accumulated wealth and provide a steady income stream.

It's crucial therefore to review your ETF portfolio periodically and make adjustments as necessitated by your changing circumstances. Also, considering the market dynamics, keeping track of your underlying ETF holdings can be insightful.

In conclusion, ETFs have proven to be an exceptional tool for retirement planning. Their versatility, efficiency, and simplicity make them an attractive addition to retirement portfolios. However, like any investment, it's essential to understand the implication of ETFs, evaluate them in the light of your personal circumstances, and seek professional advice if necessary. Their appropriate use can lead to the creation of a durable, efficient, and customizable retirement portfolio.

Chapter 11. Smart Investing: Predicting and Mitigating ETF Risks

Financial investments, while rewarding, are inherent with various layers of risk. Exchange Traded Funds (ETFs), celebrated for their flexibility, diversity, and relatively low cost, are no exceptions. This section aims to equip you with the understanding and tools necessary to narrate, predict, and mitigate the adversity and potential risks accompanying ETFs. By engaging with these concepts, you can optimize your investment strategy, molding it to accommodate and thrive amidst the unpredictable, dynamic world of investing.

11.1. Understanding the Risks

Foremost, it is crucial to understand the types of risks associated with ETF investing. It's a multi-faceted entity compromised of market risk, sector risk, liquidity risk, credit risk, and country risk.

- Market Risk: This is the general risk associated with any investment in the stock market, driven by macroeconomic factors affecting overall market movements.

- Sector Risk: Some ETFs invest in specific sectors. The performance of these funds is, therefore, susceptible to the collective performance of the industries within the sector.

- Liquidity Risk: The risk that arises when there is a paucity of market demand for an ETF. Less liquid ETFs can face price discrepancies and might be difficult to sell.

- Credit Risk: Pertains to fixed-income ETFs that invest in bonds. It represents the risk that a bond issuer could default.

- Country Risk: For ETFs that invest in foreign markets, the risk is attributed to geopolitical, economic, and financial health of the concerned country.

Identifying these risks is the first step towards managing them. Remember, every ETF carries a unique combination of these risks.

11.2. Predicting Risks

The next step in managing risks associated with ETFs is successful prediction, which essentially involves spotting market trends and shifts that might intensify or trigger these risks.

To predict market risk, monitor indicators of macroeconomic health like GDP, inflation rate, and employment data. Increased volatility may be a sign of impending risks.

Track the performance of individual sectors to predict sector risks. If a sector continually lags behind the overall market, ETFs associated with that sector might bear higher risks.

To predict liquidity risk, pay attention to the trading volumes of the ETF. Lower volumes might signal less liquidity.

For credit risk, investors could look at the credit ratings of the bonds in which the ETF invests. Falling ratings are a negative indicator.

Country risk can be deduced from political or economic instability in a nation, tariff wars or significant changes in national policy.

Remember, risk prediction isn't foolproof. The aim is to gain a nuanced understanding that can guide decisions, not guarantee outcomes.

11.3. Mitigating Risks

Just as important as detecting risks is knowing how to manage them. Herein, constructing a diversified portfolio is key.

For market and sector risks, ensure that your ETF investments are spread across different market segments and business sectors. Avoid concentrating your investments in one sector.

Liquidity risk can be managed by investing in highly traded, well-established ETFs, which have more liquidity and greater price stability.

To manage credit risk, consider ETFs containing bonds with higher, more stable credit ratings.

For country risk, diversify by geographical area, including investments from stable countries, providing a balance against the uncertainty of riskier markets.

11.4. Tools for Risk Management

Utilizing investment tools can add another layer of risk mitigation. Using stop and limit orders can help automate your risk management and mitigate losses if prices drop. Setting up a 'trailing stop order', which adjusts with the market price, can help secure gains and limit losses. Limit orders allow you to buy or sell an ETF at a specified price.

Another helpful tool is a risk management software, which can assist in assessing the overall risk profile of your portfolio. This can help you understand and adjust your strategy in real-time.

Identifying, predicting, and mitigating the various risks involved with ETF investing can help solidify your portfolio amid turbulent markets. While it is impossible to eliminate all risk, understanding and managing it can help pave the way to successful investing. Remember, intelligence, like risk, accompanies every investment decision.